The Marriage Ceremony

A Step by Step Guide for Pastors and Ministers

2nd Edition

Robert R. Thibodeau

The Marriage Ceremony
A Step by Step Guide for Pastors and Ministers

ISBN 13:   978-0692207444
ISBN 10:   0692207449

All scripture is taken from the King James Version unless otherwise noted.

Freedom Through Faith Publications
Baltimore, MD 21220

Table of Contents

Introduction

The joining together of a man and woman into marriage is one of the most sacred of our Christian Traditions. The Covenant of Marriage is symbolic of the Covenant we have with Jesus Christ. In the Bible, we are referred to as the Bride of Christ. Marriage is, therefore, very serious business. When a couple prepares to enter the Marriage Covenant, it is extremely important that all parties understand exactly what is about to happen. It is not just between the man and the woman. The purpose in the wedding party (Best Man, Maid of Honor, etc.) is to ratify and stand in agreement for the marriage. Even the families that are gathered together are to be witnesses to this union.

The tradition of Covenant goes back to Abraham's time. You should conduct your own studies on the seriousness of the Covenant. It is the joining together of two distinct people – as representatives of two distinct families – and making ONE new family! In the eyes of God, it is NOT just two people joining together. It is two FAMILIES joining together.

This book has been written from that perspective. When I conduct wedding ceremonies, I provide clear, concise instructions to all in attendance, the bride and groom, the witnesses standing up as part of the wedding ceremony and the families sitting in attendance. Everyone has a part to play in the success of the wedding.

The number one reason so many marriages fail today is probably because the church has allowed the wedding ceremony to become just that – a wedding ceremony and that is all. It is a Covenant of Marriage. It creates a new family in the eyes of God and in the eyes of the people here on earth.

My prayer is that you will find the step-by-step instructions contained in this book helpful. I have left blank spaces where the names of the Bride and Groom can be inserted. As a matter of practice, I usually use a "sticky note" cut out to fit in the space provided upon which I write in the name of the Bride and Groom (especially if there is a certain pronunciation or name they want used, i.e. Larry instead of Lawrence).

Feel free to modify and adapt the wording of the ceremonies to fit your own personal style and situational needs. I have found these three ceremonies as the most often used.

This second edition of "The Marriage Ceremony" includes a few shorter paragraphs' than originally included in the First Edition. A few "typos" were discovered that have also been corrected. I have also designed a darker cover, to fit in with the more traditional "pastor's black book" used during wedding ceremonies. Other than these minor alterations, the overall content of the book has remained the same.

Robert R. Thibodeau
2014

Chapter One: The Traditional Ceremony

THE GIVING OF THE BRIDE

To the Father: "Who gives this bride away in
                                  marriage?"

Response of the Father: "I do."

To the Groom: "Take your bride and step forward
                                  please."

To the Congregation: "I ask that you remain standing as we
                                  go before the Lord in Prayer."

Minister: "Our most gracious and Heavenly Father, we thank
     you for the privilege of being in the Body of Christ. We are
     gathered here today, to join together this man and this
     woman in the Covenant of Marriage. We are gathered here
     today to watch the miracle of Your Love and the Power of
     Your Spirit work in the lives of these two people. We give
     to you the Honor and the Glory and the Praise for the Power
     of the Holy Spirit in our lives, to bring us into a place of
     union with the Father, union with the Son and union with the
     Holy Spirit and union with one another. We thank you, in
     Jesus Mighty Name we pray. AMEN.

To the Congregation: "You may be seated."

To all present:

"Into the Holy State of Matrimony, these two people,
_____ and _____ come
now to be joined together. If any person can show just cause as to
why they may not lawfully be joined together in marriage, let them
speak now or else hereafter, forever hold their peace."

Minister:

The marriage ceremony is the closest relationship that can exist on this earth between two human beings. When a man and woman decide to enter into the Marriage Covenant, both of them should realize what that responsibility entails. Marriage is very serious business and is not to be entered into lightly.

When two born again believers know that it is God's will for them to be married, they come together before God, before a minister and before witnesses, as we have today. They then make pledges before God and before the witnesses. Pledging their lives to one another for eternity. They make these professions publically, professing their love and devotion, pronouncing vows and pledging their lives to each other.

As they publically profess these marriage vows in Faith, the Power of God then goes into operation. Before all who are gathered here to witness this beautiful ceremony, a miracle takes place right before your eyes. The couple is united by God and become ONE in His sight. Their union is threefold:

       They are joined together SPIRITUALLY by God; they are joined together LEGALLY by contract and PHYSICALY in consummating the marriage. They are forgiving each other of their past and they are now joining together and looking towards the future. They are joined together, just as Jesus is joined to the church.

It is a miraculous union. It is a miracle from God. And it takes place, right here, right now.

CHARGE TO THE BRIDE AND TO THE GROOM

_____ and _____

As I read scriptures from the fifth chapter of the Book of Ephesians, I want both of you to pay very close attention to the words stated here. They are God's own Words. Words that the Holy Spirit will honor, as we stand on them together, in Faith.

The world has the idea that marriage is simply a legal contract. It is that…but much more. At the same time you are entering this legal contract, you are also entering a Spiritual Contract. When the Words of Faith are spoken, according to God's Word, between two born again believers, the Power of God begins to operate in your lives. There is an actual miracle which takes place as the Faith of two people join together and release their Faith in God's Power. God will honor your Faith. And this Faith brings you into union together. With these thoughts in mind, listen to this scripture from Ephesians chapter five:

Wives, submit yourselves unto your husbands, as unto the Lord. Now, let me stop right here for just a second. The word "submit" does not mean to be "under" (like under subjection). The actual Greek translation is "Hupotasso" which means to line up behind or stand alongside. Basically, it means you are to support him in all he does.

That is what is meant by, Wives, submit yourselves unto your husbands as onto the Lord. For the husband is the head of the wife, even as Christ is the head of the church; and he is the Savior of the body.

Therefore, as the church is subject to Christ, so let the wives be subject to their own husbands in every thing. Husbands, LOVE your wives, even as Christ also loved the church and gave himself for it; that he might sanctify and cleanse it with the washing of water by the Word. So that he might present it to Himself as a glorious church, not having spot or wrinkle or any such thing. But that it should be Holy and without blemish.

So ought men to love their wives as their own bodies. He that loves his wife loves himself. For no man ever yet hated his own flesh; but nourishes and cherishes it, even as the Lord cares for the church;

For we are members of one body, of His flesh and of His bones.

For this cause and reason, shall a man leave his father and his mother, and shall be joined unto his wife. The two of them shall be one flesh. This is a great mystery, but I speak concerning Christ and the church. AMEN.

_____ and _____, I am now going to ask each of you a very important question. I want you to answer it truthfully and honestly before God and these witnesses. If the answer is YES – answer yes. If the answer is NO – then answer no.

To the Groom: _____ have you
                          accepted Jesus Christ as Lord and Savior?

Groom: I have.

To the Bride: _____ have you
                          accepted Jesus Christ as Lord and Savior?

Bride: I have.

(Note: if the answer is NO. Ask that person if they are ready to accept Jesus as Lord and their personal Savoir at this time. That would make for a "truly miraculous wedding." In almost 15 years of conducting weddings, though, I have never had someone answer NO to this question. I have had a couple of NO answers during pre-marriage meetings – and I was able take care of this prior to the wedding).

Minister: *To the Bride and Groom*

Upon your public confession of Faith in Jesus, you have made known to all present here, that Jesus Christ of Nazareth is your Lord and Savior. I make this announcement before this congregation and before these witnesses:

When two people join themselves together to the Lord Jesus Christ by Faith, according to God's own Word and God's own Statements, they stand cleansed – as clean before God as Adam and Eve were in the Garden of Eden prior to the fall and prior to sin entering their lives. This is not just forgiveness of sin alone. The Bible says ANY man who is in Christ has become a new creature – a new creation. Old things – the old sinful person – have passed away and all things have now become new.

A miracle took place when you made Jesus the Lord of your life. The Holy Spirit used the same Power of God that actually raised Jesus from the dead – His Creative Power – and caused your spirit to be reborn. The Holy Spirit then joined you to Jesus forever by that same Creative Power. We are about to witness this same Power of God join you to each other in marriage.

When two born again believers come before God to be joined together as husband and wife, the Apostle Paul calls it a mystery and then says, "But I speak concerning Christ and the church." When you made Jesus the Lord of your lives, you were joined to Him. First Corinthians 6:17 says you are ONE with Him. In Ephesians it says that you have become one flesh with the Lord. You are His, He is Yours. You are one, together with Him.

Do not EVER tamper with this union. The Love of God does not say, "I love you, but…"

The Love of God simply says, "I LOVE YOU." That is all it ever says. When one party does something wrong, the simple words, "I LOVE YOU" carry all of the Power of God. Do not allow the sun to go down on your wrath. Something Holy, something beyond reproach, takes place with God inside of you. It is the LOVE OF GOD.

Minister: **To the Witnesses (Wedding Party):**

I want to speak to the witnesses standing here:

Jesus said in Matthew 18, "Again, I say unto you, that if two of you shall agree on earth as touching any thing that they shall ask, it shall be done for them of my Father which is Heaven."

You are not here simply out of tradition. You have a far more important part than that. You are here for a very serious purpose. You are here to bear witness, forever, of the miracle that is about to take place right here before your very eyes. You are here to add your agreement before God, with this couple, to that which takes place.

Don't ever tamper with this agreement. Do not ever allow anyone else to tamper with this agreement. Regardless of what happens, you must always be in agreement with this union.

If you are in agreement, then so state by saying "I WILL."

Wedding Party Response: "I WILL"

Minister: **To the Congregation:**

"I now want to speak to everyone sitting here in attendance for a moment."

In the eyes of Almighty God, these two people are washed in the Blood of the Lamb, Jesus Christ of Nazareth. They have prayed and agreed together to come here, before you and before these witnesses, to be joined together as husband and wife. They believe with all of their hearts that this is the perfect Will of God for them forever. They have made their decision. So, from now until the end of time, I charge YOU to do everything in YOUR power to see that this union remains strong, happy, Holy and prosperous. Woe be to any person who would tamper with this union and cause it to be anything other than joyous and prosperous in the eyes of God. This is a miraculous thing and it IS OF GOD.

If you are in agreement, say so by stating: "WE WILL"

Congregation Response: "WE WILL"

PROFESSION OF VOWS BY THE BRIDE AND GROOM

Minister: **To the Groom**

_____, do you take this woman,
_____, as your wife, as your own flesh, to
love her even as Christ loves the Church, to protect her and care for
her; to honor and keep her, in sickness and in health; forsaking all
others, keeping yourself pure only for her, so long as you both shall
live?

Groom: I DO

Then turn to her make this profession of your Faith:

I _____, according to the Word of
God, I leave my father and my mother and I join myself to you, to
be a husband to you. From this moment forward, we shall be one.
For better or for worse; for richer, for poorer; in sickness and in
health; to love, to honor and to cherish you; till death do us part.
According to God's Holy Word – I give to you my life, forever.

Minister: **To the Bride**

_____, do you take this man
_____, as your husband, submitting
yourself to him as unto the Lord, showing reverence to him as the
head of this union; to serve him, to love him, to honor him and to
keep him. Forsaking all others and keeping yourself pure only for
him, so long as you both shall live?

Bride: I DO

Then turn to him and make this profession of your Faith:

I _____, according to the Word of
God, I join myself to you; to submit myself only to you and to be a
wife for you. From this moment forward, we shall be one. For better
or for worse; for richer, for poorer; in sickness and in health; to
love, to cherish and to honor; till death do us part. According to
God's Holy Word – I give to you my life, forever.

PRESENTATION OF RINGS

Minister: *To the Groom*

May I have the Bride's ring, please?

*(Taking the ring, the minister holds the ring up for all to see **and addresses the congregation as well as the groom**):*

A ring is a very precious thing – a token of your Faith and your love for this woman. This ring is made out of precious metal. It is a never ending circle that indicates the continuing, never ending Love of God – a Love that never fails; never presents itself as haughty or puffed up. The Love of God and the Faith of God is what causes His Power to move in your lives.

I want you to wear these rings as a continual reminder of your Faith and of these vows, which have made to each other, in front of these witnesses and in the presence of God.

The Word of God says, "Above all, take the shield of Faith, with which you shall be able to quench all the fiery darts of the wicked one." If anyone could break up this union, it would be Satan. So give him no place in your marriage. Give him NO place! And this marriage will be forever.

(Give the ring to the Groom)

Minister: *To the Groom*

Take this ring and place it on her finger. Look into her eyes and repeat after me:

With this ring, I thee wed. It is a token of my love for you and a token of my Faith, that I release now, in the Jesus Name.

Minister: *To the Bride*

May I have the Groom's ring please?

*(Taking the ring, the minister holds the ring up for all to see, **but speaks directly to the Groom, saying**):*

A ring can mean two very different things. It can be a never ending sign of your love, or it can be a shackle of bondage. I am going to charge you with a memory that you should always remember: This woman stands BY your side and not under your feet. I want you to wear these rings in remembrance that she is your partner and your helpmate.

She is not your slave - and these rings should never be a shackle of bondage. You now have the responsibility in the eyes of God to be the head of this union.

You have the Spiritual responsibility as well, in the eyes of God, for the upbringing of your family in the ways of God and in the Faith of Christ. You will ultimately answer to God for how you handle this responsibility.

Minister: *To the Bride*

I want you to place this ring on his finger with these things I have just said in your mind. There is no place in the Word of God that gives people the right to dominate one another. Your vows have stated that you submit to one another in the responsibilities of this life, expecting God and His Power to always make the difference.

(Give the ring to the Bride)

So place this ring on his finger and, as you do, look into his eyes and repeat after me:

With this ring, I thee wed. It is a token of my love for you and a token of my Faith, that I release now, in the Jesus Name.

Minister: *To the Congregation*

Let us pray:

Our Father, who art in Heaven, Holy be Thy Name. Thy Kingdom Come, Thine Will be done, on earth, as it is Heaven. Give us this day our daily bread, forgiving us of our sins as we forgive those who sin against us. Lead us not into temptation, but deliver us from all evil. For Thine is the Kingdom and the Power and the Glory – Forever and ever, in Jesus' Name, AMEN.

Now, join me as we pray a special Blessing over this couple:

O Eternal God, Creator and preserver of all mankind, giver of all Spiritual Grace, the author of Everlasting Life: send NOW, your Blessings upon these, your servants, this man and this woman, whom we Bless in Your Holy Name. That, just like Isaac and Rebecca lived Faithfully together, so this couple may surely perform and keep the vows and covenant made between them this day, whereof these rings have been given and received as a token and a pledge and may remain in perfect love and peace together, and live according to your laws – through Jesus Christ our Lord.

(Minister raises one or both hands in Blessing the couple and states):

Now, may God the Father, God the Son and God the Holy Spirit, BLESS, Preserve and Keep you: May the Lord mercifully with His Favor, look upon you and fill you with all Spiritual benediction and Grace; that you may so live together in this life and so that in the world to come, you may have Life Everlasting. In Jesus Name. AMEN.

*(If there is to be a candle lighting ceremony or mixing of colored sand – **do so now**. When completed....have them return in front of you and say):*

Minister: *To all present*

For as much as _____ and
_____ have consented to come together in
Holy Wedlock, and have witnessed the same before God and before
this congregation of witnesses, and have given and pledged their
lives each to the other, and have declared the same by the giving
and receiving of rings and by the joining of hands...

I pronounce, by the Power and Authority given to me by our Lord
and Savior Jesus Christ and recognized by the State of
_____ and these, the United States of America, I
now pronounce you one together – you are now, Husband and Wife.
You may now kiss your bride.

(As they kiss, the minister says):

What God has joined together, let no man take apart.

(After the kiss, have the couple turn towards the audience ...)

Minister: *To the Congregation*

Ladies and Gentlemen, I present to you,

Mr. and Mrs. _____
                (using the Grooms first and last name)

Chapter Two

The Civil Ceremony

The traditional wedding ceremony is held in a church, outdoors or perhaps in someone's home. Sometimes, on certain occasions, the minister may find himself or herself in a position where a civil ceremony is called for. The situations are too numerous to go into detail here, I will leave it up to the individual minister to rely on the leading of the Holy Spirit for guidance. But every minister should have a short, four or five minute ceremony available for use. This chapter is dedicated to that cause.

The Civil Ceremony

Minister: "Marriage is an institution of Divine appointment and is considered one of the most treasured and joyous occasions among civilized men. It is a very important step in life and should not be entered into lightly or without thinking of the vows you are about to take. You should only enter into marriage knowing this is a very important and legal commitment which will affect your lives forever."

"Into this estate, these two persons have now come to be joined together. If any person present can show just cause as to why they may not be lawfully joined together in marriage, let them speak now – or forever hold their peace."

Minister: ***To the Couple -***   I solemnly charge you
both, as you hope and pray for peace and joy
and love in this marriage, that you both think
one more time about what you are about to do
and about to enter into. If either one of you
know of any just cause that would prohibit
you or prevent you from legally being joined
together in marriage, I charge you to confess
it now.

Is it both of your will's then to proceed?
(both respond with "yes.")   **(tell them to join
hands together).**

Minister: ***To the Groom***

Do you, _____,
take this woman to be your lawfully wedded
wife and do you promise – before God and
before these witnesses – to love her, comfort
her, honor, keep her, cherish her, in sickness
and in health, for richer and for poorer,
forsaking all others and keeping yourself only
for her – so long as you both shall live?

Groom: "I do."

Minister: ***To the Bride***

Do you, _____
take this man to be your lawfully wedded
husband; and do you solemnly promise
before God and these witnesses that you will
love, honor, and keep him, in sickness and in
health, for richer and for poorer and keep
yourself only for him, so long as you both
shall live?

Bride: "I do."

(If the parties have a ring, the minister shall instruct the man to place the ring on the third finger of the woman's left hand and hold hands as he repeats the following after the minister...)

Minister   *(followed by the Groom repeating):*

"With this ring, I thee wed. To you I bestow
all of my worldly goods and to you I join
myself forever. In the Name of the Father,
the Son and the Holy Ghost. AMEN."

(If the woman has a ring for the man, the minister shall instruct her to place the ring on the third finger of the left hand of the man and repeat the same statement above).

Minister: *To all present...*

"In as much as this man and this woman
have, in the presence of God and these
witnesses, consented together and have
joined hands, pledged their lives and all their
worldly goods one to the other *(if rings were
exchanged:* and having declared the same by
giving and receiving these rings), I now,
according to the ordinances of God and as
authorized by the State of _____,
pronounce you one, as Husband and Wife.
What therefore God has now joined together,
let no man put asunder."

"Now, may the God of Peace prosper you,
Bless you and keep you forever in this new
relationship. May the Grace of Jesus Christ
abound unto you, now and always. Amen.
Congratulations."

"You may kiss your bride."

Minister: *(to the audience, if any):* I present to you,
Mr. & Mrs.

_____

Chapter Three

The "Episcopal Type" of Marriage Ceremony

THE GIVING OF THE BRIDE

Minister: *To the Father*   "Who gives this bride away in marriage?"

Response of the Father: "I do."

Minister: *To the Groom*   "Take your bride and step forward please."

Minister: *To the Congregation*

"I ask that you remain standing as we go before the Lord in Prayer."

Minister: "Our most gracious and Heavenly Father, we thank you for the privilege of being in the Body of Christ. We are gathered here today, to join together this man and this woman in the Covenant of Marriage. We are gathered here today to watch the miracle of Your Love and the Power of Your Spirit work in the lives of these two people. We give to you the Honor and the Glory and the Praise for the Power of the Holy Spirit in our lives to bring us into a place of union with the Father, union with the Son and union with the Holy Spirit and union with one another. We thank you, in Jesus Mighty Name we pray. AMEN.

To the Congregation: "You may be seated."

Minister: *To all present*

"Into the Holy State of Matrimony, these two people,
_____ and _____
come now to be joined together. If any person can show just cause
as to why they may not lawfully be joined together in marriage, let
them speak now or else hereafter, forever hold their peace."

Minister:

The marriage ceremony is the closest relationship that can exist on
this earth between two human beings. When a man and woman
decide to enter into the Marriage Covenant, both of them should
realize what that responsibility entails. Marriage is very serious
business and is not to be entered in to lightly.

When two born again believers know that it is God's will for them
to be married, they come together before God, before a minister and
before witnesses, as we have today. They then make pledges before
God and before the witnesses. Pledging their lives to one another
for eternity. They make these professions publically, professing
their love and devotion, pronouncing vows and pledging their lives
to each other.

As they publically profess these marriage vows in Faith, the Power
of God then goes into operation. Before all who are gathered here
to witness this beautiful ceremony, a miracle takes place right
before your eyes. The couple is united by God and become ONE in
His sight. Their union is threefold:

They are joined together SPIRITUALLY by God; they are joined
together LEGALLY by contract and PHYSICALY when the
marriage is consummated. They are forgiving each other of their
past and are joining together, looking towards the future. They are
joined together, just as Jesus is joined to the church.

It is a miraculous union. It is a miracle from God. And it takes
place, right here, right now.

CHARGE TO THE BRIDE AND TO THE GROOM

_____ and _____

As I read scriptures from the fifth chapter of the Book of Ephesians, I want both of you to pay very close attention to the words stated here. They are God's own Words, which the Holy Spirit will honor, as we stand on them together, in Faith.

The world has the idea that marriage is simply a legal contract. It is that...but more. At the same time you are entering this legal contract, you are also entering a Spiritual Contract. When the Words of Faith are spoken, according to God's Word, between two born again believers, the Power of God begins to operate in your lives. There is an actual miracle which takes place as the Faith of two people join together and release their Faith in God's Power. God will honor your Faith. And this Faith brings you into union together. With these thoughts in mind, listen to this scripture from Ephesians chapter five:

Wives, submit yourselves unto your husbands, as unto the Lord. Now, let me stop right here for just a second. The word "submit" does not mean to be "under" (like under subjection). The actual Greek translation is "Hupotasso" which means to line up behind or stand alongside. Basically, it means you are to support him in all he does."

That is what is meant by, Wives, submit yourselves unto your husbands as onto the Lord. For the husband is the head of the wife, even as Christ is the head of the church; and he is the savior of the body.

Therefore, as the church is subject to Christ, so let the wives be subject to their own husbands in every thing. Husbands, LOVE your wives, even as Christ also loved the church and gave himself for it; that he might sanctify and cleanse it with the washing of water by the Word. So that he might present it to Himself as a glorious church, not having spot or wrinkle or any such thing. But that it should be Holy and without blemish.

So ought men to love their wives as their own bodies. He that loves his wife loves himself. For no man ever yet hated his own flesh; but nourishes and cherishes it, even as the Lord cares for the church;

For we are members of one body, of His flesh and of His bones.

For this cause and reason, shall a man leave his father and his mother, and shall be joined unto his wife. The two of them shall be one flesh. This is a great mystery, but I speak concerning Christ and the church. AMEN.

_____ and _____, I am now going to ask each of you a very important question. I want you to answer it truthfully and honestly before God and these witnesses. If the answer is YES – answer yes. If the answer is NO – then answer no.

Minister: *To the Groom*
_____ have you accepted Jesus Christ as Lord and Savior?

Groom: I have.

Minister: *To the Bride*
_____ have you accepted Jesus Christ as Lord and Savior?

Bride: I have.

(Note: if the answer is NO. Ask that person if they are ready to accept Jesus as Lord and their personal Savoir at this time. That would make for a "truly miraculous wedding." In almost 15 years of conducting weddings, though, I have never had someone answer NO to this question. I have had a couple of NO answers during pre-marriage meetings – and I was able to take care of this prior to the wedding).

Minister: ***To the Bride and Groom***

Upon your public confession of Faith in Jesus, you have made known to all present here that Jesus Christ of Nazareth is your Lord and Savior. I make this announcement before this congregation and before these witnesses:

When two people join themselves together to the Lord Jesus Christ by Faith, according to God's own Word and God's own Statements, they stand cleansed – as clean before God as Adam and Eve were in the Garden of Eden prior to the fall and prior to sin entering their lives. This is not just forgiveness of sin alone. The Bible says ANY man who is in Christ has become a new creature – a new creation. Old things – the old sinful person – have passed away and all things have now become new.

A miracle took place when you made Jesus the Lord of your life. The Holy Spirit used the same Power of God that raised Jesus from the dead – His Creative Power – and caused your spirit to be reborn. The Holy Spirit then joined you to Jesus forever by that same Creative Power. We are about to witness this same Power of God join you to one another.

When two born again believers come before God to be joined together as husband and wife, the Apostle Paul calls it a mystery and then says, "But I speak concerning Christ and the church." When you made Jesus the Lord of your lives, you were joined to Him. First Corinthians 6:17 says you are ONE with Him.

In Ephesians it says that you have become one flesh with the Lord. You are His, He is yours. You are one, together with Him.

I want you to understand that if you rightly discern the Body of Christ, then you will rightly discern the miracle that takes place in marriage. Your spirits will be joined together and you will become one soul. You will not just be one in the eyes of the law. There is something much more powerful than that which is about to take place. The very Creative Power of God will join you together. The same power that joined you with Jesus when you made Him your Lord will now join both of you together.

Do not EVER tamper with this union. The Love of God does not say, "I love you, but…"

The Love of God simply says, "I LOVE YOU." That is all it ever says. When one party does something wrong, the simple words, "I LOVE YOU" carry all of the Power of God. Do not allow the sun to go down on your wrath. Something Holy, something beyond reproach, takes place with God inside of you. It is the LOVE OF GOD.

Minister: *To the Witnesses (Wedding Party)*

I want to speak to the witnesses here:

Jesus said in Matthew 18, "Again, I say unto you, that if two of you shall agree on earth as touching any thing that they shall ask, it shall be done for them of my Father which is Heaven."

You are not here simply out of tradition. You have a far more important part than that. You are here for a very serious purpose. You are here to bear witness, forever, of the miracle, which is about to take place, right here before your very eyes. You are here to add your agreement before God, with this couple, to that which takes place.

Don't ever tamper with this agreement. Do not ever allow anyone else to tamper with this agreement. Regardless of what happens, you must always be in agreement with this union.

If you are in agreement, then state so by saying "I WILL."

Wedding Party Response: "I WILL"

Minister: *To the Congregation*

"I now want to speak to everyone here for a moment."

In the eyes of Almighty God, these two people are washed in the Blood of the Lamb, Jesus Christ of Nazareth. They have prayed and agreed together to come here, before you and before these witnesses to be joined together as husband and wife. They believe with all of their hearts that this is the perfect Will of God for them, forever. They have made their decision. So, from now until the end of time, I charge YOU to do everything in YOUR power to see that this union remains strong, happy, Holy and prosperous. Woe be to any person who would tamper with this union and cause it to be anything other than joyous and prosperous in the eyes of God. This is a miraculous thing and it IS OF GOD.
If you are in agreement, say so by stating: "WE WILL"

Congregation Response: "WE WILL"

PROFESSION OF VOWS BY THE BRIDE AND GROOM

Minister: *To the Groom*

_____, do you take this woman, _____, as your wife, as your own flesh, to love her even as Christ loves the Church, to protect her and care for her; to honor and keep her, in sickness and in health; forsaking all others, keeping yourself pure only for her, so long as you both shall live?

Groom: I DO

Then turn to her make this profession of your Faith:

I _____, according to the Word of God, leave my father and my mother and I join myself to you, to be a husband to you. From this moment forward, we shall be one. For better or for worse; for richer or for poorer; in sickness and in health; to love, to honor and to cherish you; till death do us part. According to God's Holy Word – I give to you my life, forever.

Minister: *To the Bride*

_____, do you take this man
_____, as your husband, submitting yourself to him
as unto the Lord, showing reverence to him as the head of this
union; to serve him, to love him, to honor him and to keep him.
Forsaking all others and keeping yourself pure only for him, so long
as you both shall live?

Bride: I DO

Then turn to him and make this profession of your Faith:

I _____, according to the Word of
God, submit myself only to you; to be a wife for you. From this
moment forward, we shall be one. For better or for worse; for richer
or for poorer; in sickness and in health; to love, to honor and to
cherish you; till death do us part; according to God's Holy Word – I
give to you my life, forever.

PRESENTATION OF RINGS

Minister: *To the Groom*   May I have the Bride's
                                                           ring, please?

(Taking the ring, the minister holds the ring up for all to see and addresses the congregation as well as the groom):

A ring is a very precious thing – a token of your Faith and your love for this woman. This ring is made out of precious metal. It is a never ending circle that indicates the continuing, never ending Love of God – a Love that never fails, never presents itself as haughty or puffed up. The Love of God and the Faith of God is what causes His Power to move in your lives.

I want you to wear these rings as a continual reminder of your Faith and of these vows, which you have made to each other, in front of these witnesses and in the presence of God.

The Word of God says, "Above all, take the shield of Faith, with which you shall be able to quench all the fiery darts of the wicked one." If anyone could break up this union, it would be Satan. So give him no place in your marriage. Give him NO place! And this marriage will be forever.

Minister: *To the Groom*

Take this ring and place it on her finger. Look into her eyes and repeat after me:

With this ring, I thee wed. It is a token of my love for you, and a token of my Faith, that I release now, in the Jesus Name.

Minister: *To the Bride*

May I have the Groom's ring please?

(Taking the ring, the minister holds the ring up for all to see, but speaks directly to the Groom, saying):

A ring can mean two very different things. It can be a never ending sign of your love, or it can be a shackle of bondage. I am going to charge you with a memory you should always remember:

This woman stands BY your side, not under your feet. I want you to wear these rings in remembrance that she is your partner and your helpmate.

She is not your slave and these rings should never be a shackle of dominance. You now have the responsibility in the eyes of God to be the head of this union.

You have the Spiritual responsibility as well, in the eyes of God, for the upbringing of your family in the ways of God and in the Faith of Christ. You will ultimately answer to God for how you handle this responsibility.

Minister: *To the Bride*

I want you to place this ring on his finger with these things I have
just said in your mind. There is no place in the Word of God that
gives people the right to dominate one another. Your vows have
stated that you submit to one another in the responsibilities of this
life, expecting God and His Power to always make the difference.

(Hand the ring to the bride)

So place this ring on his finger and, as you do, look into his eyes
and repeat after me:

With this ring, I thee wed. I give it as a token of my love for you
and a token of my Faith. I believe with all my heart that this is
forever. It is with all my love and with all my Faith, that I release
now, in Jesus Name.

Pronouncement

Minister: *To the Bride and the Groom*

Join hands please.

As a representative of Jesus Christ, before Almighty God and in the
Name of the Father, The Son and the Holy Ghost, and with the
authority of the State of _____, I now pronounce you
as one, together. You are now, Husband and Wife.

Communion

Minister: *To the Bride and Groom*

Please kneel to receive communion together.

Both of you have received communion in the past. You know what it means. But I want to now remind you of the covenant you have just entered into and the covenant you have together with God. This covenant was ratified by the shed blood of Jesus Christ on the Cross of Cavalry. And it was for you.

Now, with you, we see something that has never existed before. When each of you were born again, you became new creatures in Christ. Now, by being joined together in marriage, you have now become a NEW creation in Christ, because out of the two – you are now ONE. When you agree on things to come – they WILL come to pass. You have God's Promises on that. You now have an awesome power at your disposal. You are going to notice a new realm of your life, beginning now, that you never dreamed possible.

The Bible says there is a spiritual law where one can put a thousand to flight, but two can put 10,000 to flight. From this day forward, your everyday life will be 10,000 times more powerful spiritually than you have ever experienced before.

It is important for you, in these first moments of your new life together, to honor the Lord for what He has done. Honor Him at His table of Covenant.

Jesus said, "This is my body, broken for you. Eat ye of it."

Give the Bread to the Couple

Minister: *To the Couple.*

He shed His precious blood for you. His body bore your sicknesses and carried your diseases. The two of you, in agreement together, have the Power of the Holy Spirit at your disposal to ward off sicknesses, diseases, the storms of life and everything that hell will use to try and destroy your marriage.

In the Name of Jesus Christ, you have the God given Faith to use the Name of Jesus for your protection and benefit. Through His broken body, you now have, in your hands, the awesome Power of God Almighty to use in behalf of your marriage.

Jesus said, "This is my blood, shed for you, that ratifies the covenant I make with you. Drink of My Blood and as often as you drink it, do so in remembrance of me."

As you drink this, I want you to remember what He has done for you, what He has provided for you and what He promises to do for you in the future. Your future with Him is bright, exciting and something to be treasured. Remember Him, remember the Power that He is making available to you. Always remember the covenant He is now entering into with you.

Give the Cup to the Couple

Minister: "Take and drink."

Minister: *To the Couple.*

"Please rise to your feet."

The Blessing of the Union

Minister: *To All Present*

Now, Galatians chapter three and versus 14 and 15 states that Christ has already redeemed us from the curse of the law so that the Blessing of Abraham is made available for us, through Jesus Christ, and that we are heirs of the promise by the Power of the Holy Spirit.

In First Peter chapter three, the Bible says a man and his wife are heirs TOGETHER of the Grace of Life.

I am now going to read to you, YOUR BLESSING, YOUR INHERITANCE, according to the Promises of God as contained in the Holy Scriptures. So listen very carefully.

According to Deuteronomy, chapter 28, ALL of these Blessings will come upon you and overtake you, IF you will listen to the voice of the Lord – Your God:

Blessed shalt thou be in the city, and blessed shalt thou be in the field. Blessed shall be the fruit of thy body, and the fruit of thy ground, and the fruit of thy cattle, the increase of thy kine, and the flocks of thy sheep. Blessed shall be thy basket and thy store. Blessed shalt thou be when thou comest in, and blessed shalt thou be when thou goest out.

The LORD shall cause thine enemies that rise up against thee to be smitten before thy face: they shall come out against thee one way, and flee before thee seven ways.

The LORD shall command the blessing upon thee in thy storehouses, and in all that thou settest thine hand unto; and he shall bless thee in the land which the LORD thy God giveth thee. The LORD shall establish thee a holy people unto himself, as he hath sworn unto thee, if thou shalt keep the commandments of the LORD thy God, and walk in his ways. And all people of the earth shall see that thou art called by the name of the LORD; and they shall be afraid of thee.

And the LORD shall make thee plenteous in goods, in the fruit of thy body, and in the fruit of thy cattle, and in the fruit of thy ground, in the land, which the LORD swore unto thy fathers to give thee. The LORD shall open unto thee his good treasure, the heaven to give the rain unto thy land in his season, and to bless all the work of thine hand: and thou shalt lend unto many nations, and thou shalt not borrow.

And the LORD shall make thee the head, and not the tail; and thou shalt be above only, and thou shalt not be beneath; if that thou hearken unto the commandments of the LORD thy God, which I command thee this day, to observe and to do them.

Presentation to the Congregation

Minister: *To the Congregation:*   "Let us pray:"

Our Father, who art in Heaven, Holy be Thy Name. Thy Kingdom
Come, Thine Will be done, on earth, as it is Heaven. Give us this
day our daily bread, forgiving us of our sins just as we forgive those
who sin against us. Lead us not into temptation, but deliver us
from all evil. For Thine is the Kingdom and the Power and the
Glory – Forever and ever, in Jesus' Name, AMEN.

Now, join me as we pray a special Blessing over this couple:

O Eternal God, Creator and preserver of all mankind, giver of all
Spiritual Grace, the author of Everlasting Life: send NOW, your
Blessings upon these, your servants, this man and this woman,
whom we Bless in Your Holy Name. That, just like Isaac and
Rebecca lived Faithfully together, so this couple may surely
perform and keep the vows and covenant made between them this
day, whereof these rings have been given and received as a token
and a pledge. And may they remain in perfect love and peace
together, and live according to your laws – through Jesus Christ our
Lord. Amen.

(Minister raises both hands in Blessing the couple and states):

Now, may God the Father, God the Son and God the Holy Spirit,
BLESS, Preserve and Keep you: May the Lord mercifully with His
Favor, look upon you and fill you with all Spiritual benediction and
Grace; that you may so live together in this life and so, that in the
world to come, you may have Life Everlasting. In Jesus Name.
AMEN.

(Have the couple turn around and face the audience and say):

Minister: *To the Congregation*

Ladies and Gentlemen, I present to you,

Mr. and Mrs.

(using the Grooms first and last name)

About the Author

Pastor Robert Thibodeau

Pastor Robert Thibodeau (Pastor Bob) is the Founder and Director of "Freedom Through Faith Ministries" (FTFM.org) and is actively involved with our outreach ministry called "Mission For America."

Mission For America is a Spiritual Warfare Ministry. Pastor Bob holds public (usually outdoor) prayer meetings in specific geographic and spiritually symbolic locations around this nation. He the prays against and binds "demonic powers, wicked spirits in high places, rulers of the darkness of this world and against princes and principalities and powers in the air" (Ephesians 6) that are operating in the spiritual atmosphere of this nation and influencing leaders at all levels, both elected and appointed.

He then prays for the leaders of this land and prays for their salvation and leads the prayer of Second Chronicles 7:14. Pastor Bob then leads the public proclamation that "Jesus is Lord over the United States of America!" These meetings are video taped, edited and then placed on the "Mission For America" website *(mission4america.com)* as well as on YouTube.

Pastor Bob is also the Founder / Director of the "Freedom Through Faith Radio Network" (www.FTFRadioNetwork.com). FTFRN has three radio stations currently playing 24 hours per day.

Freedom Through Faith Christian Radio (FTFCR) is currently rated in the TOP 4% of all online Christian Talk / Sermon radio stations in the world, with listeners in over 100 different countries. Through this online radio station, smaller ministries have an opportunity to minister the Word of God to the World on an offering basis (no set fees). This allows us to *"Empower Others to Impact Their World with the Gospel of Jesus Christ."* Any ministry desiring to broadcast their recorded programs on FTFCR may set the offering price they value their own program at...even $1 per month! No other ministry offers this type of exposure on an offering basis! For more information, please visit **www.FTFChristianradio.com**

The "Praise and Worship Radio" station plays a full spectrum of Christian music genre 24 hours per day. "Praise and Worship Radio" is rated in the Top 8% of all online Christian music stations in the world. We allow independent Christian artists and musicians the opportunity to play their music on our station for a one time offering of $5...and this allows their music to be heard world wide up to 5 times per day - everyday - with no additional offerings required. For more information, please visit **www.FTFRadioNetwork.com**

"Evangelism Radio" is our latest online radio station. This station is designed to support *LIVE BROADCAST MINISTRY* - 24 hours per day! Almost one year in the making, Evangelism Radio allows those ministries desiring to enter *LIVE BROADCAST MINISTRY* to do so at very affordable rates. For just $10 per month, a ministry may broadcast LIVE one 30 minute broadcast each week; our most expensive plan allows a ministry to broadcast 60 minutes each day and every day - 7 days per week - for only $80 per month!

"Evangelism Radio" also has its own phone line support that allows a broadcaster, from anywhere in the nation, to have their listeners call in LIVE and interact with the broadcaster. This phone support is provided FREE to the broadcaster (though some listeners calling in may have to pay for long distance charges if they are not using VOIP technology - but there is NO CHARGE to the broadcaster). For more information, please visit **www.evangelismradio.com**

More information on "Freedom Through Faith Radio Network," and detailed information on all of the radio stations, can be found at **www.FTFRadioNetwork.com.**

Special Meetings and Invitations to Speak:

Pastor Bob's unique style of preaching includes lively, spiritual lessons, straight from the Word of God. He always includes a special prayer session for the sick and those needing healing or deliverance. In these prayer sessions, God confirms the Word just preached with signs and miracles.

These meetings are held on an offering basis for both large groups and small churches. Pastor Bob has preached in services with only 5 people and also in sessions involving 5,000 attendees. But he preaches with the same intensity and Love of God for both small and large.

There are no set fees for Pastor Bob to come and minister to your group, church or special meeting. All we ask for is the opportunity to accept a love offering for our ministry and the ability to sell books and CD's in the lobby or designated area before and after the service.

It is important to note that Pastor Bob receives NO salary or other compensation from this ministry. ALL offerings go directly to work in assisting Pastor Bob and this ministry in our Mission to "Get The Word Out!"

To schedule Pastor Bob, or to receive more information on his ministry, please visit our main website at **www.FTFM.org**.

BE BLESSED IN ALL YOU DO!

Freedom Through Faith Ministries
PO Box 4936
Baltimore, MD 21220
www.FTFM.org

Made in the USA
Monee, IL
06 October 2024

67310204R00038